WAKE UP TO PRAISE

The Power Of Prayer
Testimonies from a Prayer group of Christians

Author: **Wilma Brumfield-Lofton**
Co-author: **Elder Shirley Rice**

To order additional copies of this book, contact:
Xlibris
844-714-8691
www.Xlibris.com
Orders@Xlibris.com

KJV
Scripture quotations marked KJV are from the Holy Bible,
King James Version (Authorized Version).
First published in 1611.
Quoted from the KJV Classic Reference Bible,
Copyright © 1983 by The Zondervan Corporation.

ISBN: Softcover   978-1-6641-4836-9
         Hardcover   978-1-6641-4835-2
         EBook   978-1-6641-4834-5

Print information available on the last page

Library of Congress Control Number: 2020925432

Rev. date: 02/03/2021

WAKE UP TO
PRAISE

The Power Of Prayer
Testimonies from a Prayer group of Christians

Author Wilma Brumfield-Lofton
Co-Author Elder Shirley Rice
Illustrations by Andre' Brumfield
Cover Design by Felicia Benton

Thou crownest the year with thy goodness; and thy paths drop fatness.
Psalm 65:11 (KJV)

May God Bless you and your family with Happiness, Good health, Prosperity, Comfort, Love, Success, Favor, Favor and More Favor!!!
IN THE NAME OF JESUS.

Let your light so shine before men, that they may see your good works and glorify your Father in heaven.
Matthew 5-16 (KJV)

Working For God's Kingdom knowing and serving God

Table of Contents

The History

History of Wake Up To Praise

In January 2016, Sister Wilma had just completed the Daniel Fast. It was put in her thoughts to start a Prayer Call for people who could not get out to Church during the week. This call would be every Monday at 8:00 am CST.

In March 2016, Elder Shirley Rice joined our Prayer Group. She Blessed us with the name Wake Up To Praise and went to Crown Point, Indiana to legally get the rights to that name. Later we started a Bible Study Class on Thursday evenings at 7:00 pm CST.

Elder Shirley taught our first class, and Minister Adrienne Watson taught our second class. Every week we would have a different pastor speak from other states. Among them was Lady Pat's husband, Bishop Alfonso Boone. One day Lady Pat asked Pastor Patterson if he would teach our Bible Study Class, he said yes! We Thank God that Pastor Patterson has continued to teach along with Elder Shirley, empowering us with God's News!! We are thankful to God for Blessing us with such dedicated and anointed teachers. We appreciate and thank Lady Pamela Patterson and Brother Larry Rice for always allowing their spouses to take time out of their busy schedules to Bless us with God's Word.

WUTP: 351-999-4991

Mission Statement

WUTP Mission Statement

"To pray with others and share Jesus with others!"

In the same way, let your light shine before others, that they may see your good deeds and glorify your Father in heaven.

Matthew 5:16

Biography

Authors Bio

Wilma Brumfield-Lofton

Growing up in Gary, Indiana, my parents Samuel and Julia Peavy always taught me, my four brothers and sister the importance of hard work and keeping God first. They taught us to always do our best and give our best! It is those timeless lessons that I have instilled into my own son and daughter. After college, I held various office and sales positions which I enjoyed and prospered from, now retired, I reside in Missouri City, Texas. I enjoy spending time with my three grandsons, great granddaughter, blessing family, friends, and others. I was recently asked: "Considering all the things that you have done, all the things that you are doing and all of your gifts and talents, given the opportunity what are two things that you would like to do most?" Suddenly and without hesitation or consideration, clothing design and writing children's books rushed to the forefront of my thoughts and totally dominated all other considerations. It was at that point I realized it is time for me to fulfill my dreams, by utilizing and maximizing the gifts that God has placed in me and enjoy the fruit of fulfilled purpose.

Immediately I started writing my first book "Heavenly Rewards," this book offers a Christian based interactive parent-child reading experience. As of July 30, 2020, my second book "5 Crowns" has been published and can be purchased at Amazon, Barnes & Nobles and Xlibris Bookstore. I have two more children books that will be released in a few weeks. This "Wake Up To Praise" book has been a joy to write with every member expressing what our group family means to them. "Teamwork Makes The Dream Work!" It is a joy to Wake Up To Praise!

Biography
Co-Authors Bio

Elder Shirley Rice

On a cold, windy, snowy night, and my soon to be parents, Arthur and Ruby Leavell, had gone to see a scary movie; all I know is that it was frightening. Shortly after leaving the theatre, they returned home to settle in for the night. Little did my mother know, that was not going to be the case. Ruby started having contractions in the late-night hour, and by early January 4, she had given birth to a healthy bouncing baby girl given the name "Shirley Ann Leavell." There is no doubt that they were ecstatic to have a girl to join their union. My parents even entered me into a contest for The Most Beautiful Baby, and I placed first. How exciting that must have been for them. Moving forward, by the time I was five years old, I found myself in the first grade at Earlington (JW Million) elementary school. I learned quickly to study and keep up because I would have to sit out until I turned six years old if I fell behind. No way was I going to allow that to happen. I did everything my teacher Ms. Murphy asked me to do. I remember so well the first day of class. My parents walked with me to school. Later, after I had learned my route to school, I was able to walk with the other children and my big brother Walter who is two years older. By the time I was twelve years old, I was beginning my freshman year in High School. I completed all grade levels at JW Million High School, except for my senior year. It was bittersweet because my junior year would mark the last African-American class at JW Million High School.

As I learned about my new classmates, I found them to be enlightened. We studied together and found out about our cultural differences. My best subject was always English Composition and Music Appreciation. We graduated with a class of approximately thirty people. I must say that all of the fears and anxiety dissipated. I thank God for the Bible Believing parents who always prayed, made sure all of my siblings were baptized, and were taught the right things in life.

My most rewarding moment was being baptized at the young age of eight years old. I went on to attend several Colleges and Universities throughout the years. I worked for many years for the State of Indiana in Social Services, Mental Health, and as an Advocate for Children; the list goes on. I graduated from American Baptist College (ABC) and Veritas Theological Seminary. I was ordained Elder Shirley Rice in September 2009. Little did I realize that I would find such joy and fulfillment in the Ministry. I currently serve as Associate Pastor at Liberty Baptist Church, where Pastor Antwon Brown is the lead pastor. He has blessed my life in so many ways. Thank you, Pastor, for allowing God to work in your life about things concerning me.

Minister Leaders

Teachers

Wilma Brumfield-Lofton
Missouri City, Texas
MC & Prayer Request Leader

Lady Cleopatra
East Orange, New Jersey
Inspiration & Prayer

Pastor Morris Patterson
Memphis, Tennessee
Bible Study Teacher

Avis Price
Gary, Indiana
Greeter

Deacon Bobbie Stubblefield / *Wife Nicole*
Merrillville, Indiana
Praise Report Leader

Sister Connie Smith
Houston, Texas
Scripture, Song & Card Ministry

Elder Shirley Rice
Gary, Indiana
Bible Study Teacher
Intercessory Prayer Leader

Minister Leaders
Teachers

Spiritual Mother Marietta Jordan

My path to Wake Up To Praise was through Sister Wilma Lofton. I had not long move to Huntington Apartments. I did not know anyone, but one morning I opened my door to put my trash out, and along came a God-sent woman named Wilma Lofton. We became friends, and if you know anything about sister Wilma, that was easy because she is a loving and kind person. Not long after our meeting, I was in a car accident, and this sweet lady came to my rescue. Wilma did so many nice things for me. One day she gave me a card with the phone number to Wake Up To Praise. And that is how I became acquainted with all my current Christian family. My spiritual life has changed for the better. I was wearing a neck brace on our first Retreat. Elder Shirley Rice and all the wonderful Christians continued to pray for my healing, and the Lord answered our prayers. I can genuinely say that this is one of the best and most blessed Christian family I have ever been a part of. I love every member, and I thank my Lord and Savior for Wake Up To Praise. I became a part of our Bible study group on Thursday evenings. I am so thankful to God for our teachers, Pastor Morris Patterson and Elder Shirley Rice. God sent us true Christian Leaders and teachers.

Praise Glory and Honor to You Almighty God for your Goodness and Mercy. All people's strength consists of finding out the way God is going and follow going that way too.

We look forward to our Spiritual Mother's "Words Of Wisdom" Every Monday Morning!

Minister Leaders

Core Group Members

Lady Cleopatra Boone /
Husband Alfonso

Sister Sharon Haymon /
Husband William

Sister Wilma Brumfield-
Lofton

Sister
Avis Price

Elder Shirley Rice /
Husband Larry

Sister Connie Smith

Deacon Bobbie Stubblefield /
Wife Nicole

Sister Joycelyn Tucker

Sister Wilma Brumfield-Lofton

Spiritual Mother Marietta Jordan

Sister Lady Cleopatra Boone

Wake Up To Praise Call

Sister Julia Peavy

Sister Sharon Haymon

Sister Iceal Peavy

Sister Avis Price

Lady Frances-Hart

Sister Denise Bowlin -Shaffer

WUTP CHARTER MEMBERS

Wake Up To Praise Bible Study

*Sister Wilma
Brumfield-Lofton*

*Spiritual Mother
Marietta Jordan*

*Sister Lady
Cleopatra Boone*

Sister Julia Peavy

Sister Sharon Haymon

Sister Iceal Peavy

Sister Avis Price

*Lady Frances
Fulton -Hart*

*Sister Denise
Bowlin-Shaffer*

Sister Joycelyn Tucker

*Sister Elder
Shirley Rice*

*Sister Sheila James
Thomas- Prophetess*

Minister Dorothy Murray

Rosenberg, Texas

Praise the Lord!!! I am Minister Dorothy Murray. I have been a member of Wake Up To Praise since 2019. It is a blessing to wake up in the morning and give God the first fruit of your lips because He is worthy and He is altogether lovely! I love communicating with people of like passion who love the Lord. We are helpers one of another, and He gets glory when His people praise Him for who He is. It is a blessing to share your testimony with others because you don't know who you are helping. You did not go through for yourself, but to encourage and help others. Someone else is going through the same thing that God just brought you through. "We overcome by the blood of the Lamb and the words of our testimony." Rev.12:11. That is why I love being a part of Wake up To Praise. God Bless you, sisters, and brothers.

Elder Marlon & Evangelist Samantha Peavy

Norfolk Virginia

We both have hectic schedules doing God's Kingdom work, but we take time out on Thursday evenings to join the Wake Up To Praise Bible study. Pastor Morris Patterson and Elder Shirley Rice's teaching gets "Gooder and Gooder every week!" My Mother use to look forward to the Wake Up To Praise Bible studies on Thursday evening! We miss her dearly, and I know the Wake Up To Praise family misses her as well!

Evangelist Denise Moore

Missouri City, Texas

I was very excited when I went to the Retreat. I had a fantastic time with each and everyone one especially seeing the faces with the voices on Wake Up To Praise and Bible study. Everyone was so lovely and kind, and we had a hallelujah time. I experienced driving to Hamilton, Indiana. Thank you very much. 🖤 😄

Deacon Bobbie Stubblefield

Merrillville, Indiana

I was introduced to the Wake Up To Praise family by Elder Shirley Rice. Elder Rice and her husband, Larry, attends the same church as my wife Nicole and I, Liberty Baptist, with the Anointed Pastor Antwon Brown and First Lady Jennifer. I'm so excited and grateful to be a part of the Wake Up To Praise family. I look forward to and enjoy our calls; they are inspirational and spirit-filled! May God Continue To Bless Wake Up To Praise!

Elder Shirley Rice

Gary, Indiana

In March of 2016, I received a call from a very dear friend Wilma Lofton who told me about the prayer line that she had started. She asked me if I would lead prayer for the group, and I immediately said yes! I did not think much about it, but later as I began to pray over the request, I suddenly realized what an extraordinary undertaking this would be. I prayed and asked God to strengthen me and give me what to say concerning his people. Little did I realize that this was a setup for the many things that would spring forth from this prayer line. I have truly been blessed to be a blessing to the people of God. Many people are going through hardships, unemployment, marital and other relationships, disobedient children, problems with their jobs, seeking career changes, and having issues with a close friend. Some are wondering if it is time to let go and move forward. And some seek prayer against civil unrest, brutality, and domestic violence. There are so many prayer requests offered up and so many prayers answered. I did not realize what I was handed, but when you let go and allow God to work, "He Works."

I have met people by face or airwaves who are delightful and filled with the "HOLY SPIRIT." Sis. Wilma then asked me about Bible study every Thursday evening. At the time, I said yes, as long as it did not interfere with our Liberty Baptist Bible study on Wednesday evening. The first six to eight Bible studies were done by yours truly, but as we grew, other Pastors alternated weekly. Then came Pastor Morris Patterson, who agreed to teach alongside, and the rest is history. To have a seasoned man of God is an honor. Only God can do what no man can do.

We finally had an opportunity to meet one another at our First Retreat Conference in May of 2018. At the conference, which was spectacular, people came from near and afar. My pastor, Pastor Antwon Brown, delivered a sermon out of this world. We were able to put the names to the faces whenever we heard their voices. It is a privilege to be a part of Wake Up To Praise, where the prayers and the word of God is marching forward. In Your Service.

Pastor Morris Patterson

Memphis, Tennessee

The Word in Philippians 4:8 states, "Whatsoever things are true, whatsoever things are honest, whatsoever things are just, whatsoever things are pure, whatsoever things are lovely, and whatsoever things are of a good report... think on these things." These paraphrased words express the heartfelt sentiment in my soul. People are searching for answers to many questions concerning this life and the life to come. The Wake Up To Praise family is there to show love and compassion in so many ways. In personal communications through prayers, prophecies, and promises from God's Word, we share a deep-seated need for fellowship and communion. My life has been wonderfully impacted by the atmosphere of heaven I experience from being a part of Wake Up To Praise. The life lessons learned has been a unique treasure of blessings to my soul.

Thank you so much, Wake Up To Praise, for being in my life. I love you, I bless you, and I thank God for you. Your Brother in Christ, Pastor Morris Patterson.

Lady Pamela Patterson

Memphis, Tennessee

Every person needs spiritual advisors. They need wisdom delivered in love. They need to be and feel appreciated for being a fellow laborer in our Master's vineyard. Support is being with believers who are willing to share, produce, love, and understand the teachings of Jesus Christ. We are Christians allowed to experience together praise and worship. We are being taught the Word of God and devouring it like manna from heaven. One thing that has helped me through our study of the Word was answering one of my premier life questions. What is the difference between Praise and Worship? During our group study, the answer was explained clearly. My husband, Pastor Morris Patterson, and Elder Shirley Rice are outstanding teachers.

PRAISE: This is something we share with everyone, any believer, who celebrates the blessings, teachings, examples, and experiences of the glory and the majesty of Jesus Christ, our Savior and our God.

WORSHIP: True Worship is private. It is reserved strictly between me and Jesus Christ, my God ALONE. I am communing with God in my soul. You see, my soul is a space where only God and I can occupy. Thank you, my wonderful Wake Up To Praise Prayer family, for shedding light in the darkness when the world makes things look dim. Thank you for reminding me to look to the hills from whence cometh my help. All my help comes from the Lord. Your sweet spirit and prayers are proof that my God sends me unmerited grace. Be blessed, my sister Angels, and my Godly brothers. Yours, in Service to the Father, Son, and Holy Ghost, Lady Pamela Patterson.

Huntsville, Alabama

Evangelist Viola Lipscomb

I have always believed the most valuable resource we can possess is to have a spirit-filled life and partners. I was talking to my friend Sister Virginia Mattox whom I met in 1979 in Huntsville, Alabama. Sister Virginia told me about a prayer group called Wake Up To Praise and that the group had been a great blessing to her. She invited me to call in and participate in the prayer line. The prayer group has encouraged me so much. The group consists of sisters and brothers in Christ from all across the United States. We need prayer support groups like Wake Up to Praise in our communities. The group members blessed me with their words of encouragement and prayers. Listening to the trials and challenges they faced and God meeting their needs has helped me know and understand that God is no respecter of persons and always be there for me. There is power in unity prayer of agreement. I thank God for Wake Up to Praise. I thank God for Sister Virginia's continued prayers and support over the many years I have known her. She always had words of encouragement for me. We have met and prayed many times and have seen the mighty hand of God move on our behalf about our family members.

Thanks to all the prayer group's faithful servants for letting God use your talents, voices, commitments, and faithfulness. Thank you for the building up of God's Kingdom. "We are members of the body of Christ and individually members of one another even though we have different gifts." Rom. 12:4-6 (NKJV). We stand together in prayer and praise unto our God for the many gifts He has given us to glorify Him. I love each one of you. Thank you for including me as a member of Wake Up to Praise.

Minister Adrienne D. Watson

Chicago, Illinois

Wake Up To Praise means a connection with women and men of God who are willing to bare their souls and their life's issues with family and loved ones while still offering up prayers for others. It is a safe place to rest on Monday morning, waiting to hear the testimony of others about how good God is or asking for wisdom, guidance, and strength to make it through any trial. Some mornings, you almost can not wait to get on the line to tell of God's goodness in your life. It can also turn into a revelation of Bible stories and how they apply to our everyday lives. I never feel as though we can not express what we are thinking and feeling. It just may help somebody. In other words, no egos in the room! The women and men of WUTP are committed to serving and obeying God and learning more of Him. I thank Elder Shirley Rice for inviting me to be a part of the first WUTP Conference that my sister and I participated in and enjoyed. The warmth and love from the event stayed with me, and I am thankful for all the participants I met and continue to fellowship with to this day. I am incredibly grateful for Sis. Wilma Lofton for being that light so needed in our churches, homes, and today's world. Her generosity and obedience to God are unmatched, with her vision for the group that is boundless. Thank God for WUTP in all that it brings! Minister Adrienne D. Watson

Cleopatra "Lady Pat" Boone

East Orange, New Jersey

A few years ago, a friend that I so affectionately call Lady Wilma started a prayer group, which was later named WAKE UP TO PRAISE, a name that was given by our Elder Shirley Rice. I found myself rising early to get in with a community of women and men that share encouragement and hope as we are guided on the right road. So, what does Wake Up To Praise mean to me? It means I can worship with a great community of believers, and I get to be encouraged by our Spiritual Mother, Marietta. I hear scripture and song to soothe the soul and chat with my sisters and brothers. So, I am delighted to say that it means I worship in love, I am alive to see another day, I am kept alert by friendship and energized after listening, I am in unity, and can praise God without hindrance. I get to touch lives without touching in person, to open up my heart and be understood without judgment, and to keep a constant prayer as we pray for the sick. I rejoice with the praise reports and say Hallelujah. I interject that indeed our God is real because He energizes, He excites, Delivers, and sets free. Also, we close with fervent prayer from our Elder Shirley Rice, as she cries and labors in prayer for the whole community and others. I praise God for this community of warriors on the battlefield for the Lord. I praise God for the Sparkle who started this community and ends with "May God shower you with peace, protection, favor, favor and more favor, in the mighty name of Jesus Christ." And in that sweet jolly voice, she says, "I love you all, Be Blessed Everyone!"

Evangelist Mary Spratt

Aberdeen, Mississippi

Greetings in the matchless name of Jesus Christ!! I greet you as a woman of God who loves God!! I was introduced to this remarkable ministry known as Wake Up To Praise in May of 2018 by a sister and friend named Missionary Annie Davis. When she gave me the information about this unique ministry, I said WOW!! And my answer was, "Why, Yes!" I want to be a part of that. We started making plans right away to attend Wake Up To Praise's first Retreat!! Well, that was how it all got started for me. I got to the Retreat, and it was just incredible from start to finish. I got a chance to meet so many of my wonderful Sisters and Brothers in Christ Jesus. My heart rejoiced throughout my stay. On Monday mornings and Thursday evenings, Wake Up To Praise is an extraordinary blessing when I can tune in. Praise is a massive portion of my life because I owe it all to God. I am looking forward to seeing what the future holds for this great ministry, and I am praying that God will continue to allow all of the members to be a part of this great vision with many blessings added to our lives daily!! Thanks, Evangelist Mary Spratt

Sheila James Thomas Prophetess

Gary, Indiana

I want to thank Elder Shirley Rice for introducing me to the Wake Up To Praise Christian group. It has been an honor to be with like-minded believers. Being a part of Wake Up To Praise has ignited my love for Jesus Christ and His powerful Word, and for that, I am grateful! I look forward to feeding my spirit man on our Monday morning Wake Up To Praise and Thursday evening Bible study. Hearing the Testimonies of other believers has given me new hope in some of my life's challenges. In thanking "Abba, Father" for the free spirit of our CEO Wilma Lofton, Spiritual Mother Marietta Jordan, Chaplin Elder Shirley Rice, Pastor Patterson, and so many others, I don't have room to write. Bestow Blessings and continue to shower all of us with favor!

Aberdeen, Mississippi

Sister Louise Jones

I was very excited when I attended the Wake Up To Praise Retreat. I had a fantastic time with everyone, especially seeing the faces with the voices on Wake Up To Praise and Bible study calls. Everyone was so sweet and kind we had a Hallelujah Good Time!!! It was a great experience driving to Hammond, Indiana, and well worth It!

A Special Thank you to my Wake Up To Praise family. 🖤

Griffith, Indiana

Sister Cyrina Jackson

I was invited to attend the Wake Up To Praise Retreat by Elder Shirley Rice. We both are members of Liberty Baptist Church. Our pastor, Antwon Brown, was one of the speakers. I had a wonderful time and enjoyed every moment from beginning to end. It was beautiful fellowshipping with this fantastic group of Believers! I am now a member of the Wake Up To Praise family!

Memphis, Tennessee

Sister Elsie McGregor

My Niece Pamela Patterson invited me to the Wake Up To Praise Bible study call where her husband, Pastor Morris Patterson, and Elder Rice teaches God's awesome word. I have learned so much from their outstanding teaching. They take their time instructing in such a way that even a child could understand. I love the fact that at the end of their lesson, we can ask questions. They take time to explain. When I get off the Bible study call, I feel so empowered with God's Word! On Monday mornings, I look forward to our Wake Up To Praise call. It is so wonderful hearing all the voices from different states. I look forward to meeting everyone at our upcoming Retreat and put a face to the voices!

Houston, Texas

Sister Annie Cheatum

I am truly blessed to be a member of the Wake Up To Praise family! I look forward to our Monday morning call as well as our Thursday evening Bible study. We have people from different states participating. I had the opportunity to fellowship with the Texas Members. We had a luncheon at Pappadeaux Seafood Kitchen, the food was delicious, and the fellowship was Glorious! What a great group of Christians!

I am looking forward to meeting the other outstanding members at our upcoming Retreat! I pray for God's continued blessings to our Wake Up To Praise family.

Aberdeen, Mississippi

Sister Laura Dobbs

My sister Annie Davis invited me to a Wake Up To Praise call. I enjoyed It!!! I felt blessed, empowered, and inspired! I decided to join the Wake Up To Praise family. It doesn't matter how far apart we are. The Lord still reaches us. His word says, "When two or three assemble together, He is in the midst of them." Matthew 18:20. He has all of us covered in His blood.

Gary, Indiana

Darcel "Lady D" Strickland

Wilma Lofton introduced me to Wake Up To Praise, and I love being a part of our Monday morning praise group.

I enjoyed the Retreat in Hammond, Indiana. It was exciting from the beginning to the end!!! The meal was fantastic, and the Awards Night Trophy Ceremony was outstanding. Very enjoyable! Pastor Brown, who spoke at the Circle Of Prayer, is very young, but he delivered a powerful message from the Lord! He gave us what everyone needed to hear and live by. We also took a trip to St. John, Indiana, to The Shrine Of Christ's Passion, it was so very life-like, and I will never forget that incredible experience!

Sister Juanita Green

Pittsburg, Kansas

I was invited to a Wake Up To Praise call by my longtime friend Wilma Lofton. To my surprise, there was another long time friend on the call by the name of Avis Price. We all grew up together in Gary, Indiana, and attended the same church. Now we are together again with the Wake Up To Praise family. I enjoy being on the calls with this magnificent group of believers. I feel motivated and empowered by the speakers, and the power-filled prayers lead by Elder Shirley Rice. One day my husband Russell was off work and joined me on the Wake Up To Praise call. He enjoyed every moment! I am happy to be a member of this caring group of Christians.

Sister Wanda Davis

Houston, Texas

Wilma Lofton invited me to the Wake Up To Praise call. She and I worked together for years for the same company in sales. I enjoyed being on the call. It was inspirational, and the prayer was powerful! It was just what I needed to start my day and my week! I am happy to be a part of this great group of believers.

Sister Willie Kelley

Missouri City, Texas

I enjoy Thursday night Bible study "WOW!" What joy to learn more about the Lord through His word as taught by such excellent teachers, Pastor Patterson and Elder Shirley. Hopefully, as you read this book, it will raise the question about whether or not "you" have accepted Jesus Christ as your Lord and Saviour. "Oh, give thanks unto the Lord, for He Is Good: for His Mercy Endureth Forever." Psalm 107:1

Missouri City, Texas

Sister Climmie Kirkwood

It is a joy to wake up every Monday morning to praise God. To hear my sisters and brothers giving praises to God. I am so thankful for Wake Up To Praise. Like my Deacon, Bobbie says, "When praises go up, blessings come down." You may be feeling down before you get on the phone line, but I guarantee you a lifted spirit by the time you get off the phone. I enjoy hearing Sister Connie sing and Elder Shirley praying for everyone. Oh, what can I say about our Spiritual Mother? She is a woman of faith, imparting into us so much wisdom. Sister Wilma, the host of Wake Up To Praise, is always a delight when hearing her sweet voice every Monday morning. I am glad God put it on her heart to start the Wake Up To Praise call line. It has indeed been a blessing to me.

Aberdeen, Mississippi

Sister Annie Davis

Wake Up To Praise has been a Blessing to me. I have met many new Christian sisters and brothers with caring hearts and receiving minds, all reaching the same goal. My sisters and brothers will pray for you, call you, send you a greeting card, and always be ready to meet the need even though they don't see you. They are like soldiers in the army. I was introduced to WUTP by my cousin Wilma Lofton and was also invited to the Retreat. I accepted the invitation but was not sure if I was going to be able to go. I never told her no, but God saw it fit for me to go. I drove my vehicle and took with my friends Evangelist Mary Spratt and Sister Louise Jones from Aberdeen, Mississippi. We had a Spiritual Blast! I am looking forward to the upcoming WUTP Retreat to Fellowship with my family. I enjoy all my phone calls and text from Elder Shirley Rice and Ms. Wilma Lofton with much love. I introduced my sister Ms. Laura Dobbs to my WUTP family. She just fell in love with everyone and has gained a family as well!

Sister Claudette Ayers

Galveston, Texas

I want to thank WUTP from the bottom of my heart for being a part of my life when making a significant change in my life. It was 2017, the year when hurricane Harvey visited Houston with its destruction to people's lives and properties. Even though I did not have property damage, there was a considerable amount of rebuilding in my life financially and spiritually. It was at that time when I joined the WUTP prayer line.

I started working on becoming a Claims Adjuster working specifically on catastrophe storm claims around the country. I asked WUTP to pray for me as I traveled to Dallas and Fort Worth, Texas, and Mobile, AL, for training and certifications. Praise the Lord for the anointed prayer of agreement from Elder Shirley and the prayer covering from all the saints on the WUTP line. I successfully became a licensed and certified Claims Adjuster in 10 states, including the coveted New York Adjuster's License. You had to take a challenging test for the New York Adjuster's License, and I passed it on my first try. Thank you, Jesus, and my WUTP family.

In 2018, my faith was being tried financially, spiritually, emotionally, physically, and psychologically. I started traveling more to work on claims for new storms. I moved out of my beautiful home to stay with a friend to make it easier for me to travel all across the United States working on claims. I did not know that the hostess of that home would usher me into my divine destiny by not being very nice to me. My patience, love walk, and faith in God were truly tested, but again, my WUTP extraordinary prayer covering would help me to make it through the "valley of the shadow of death." I realized it was a love test for me to pass. Thank you, Jesus; I passed because of the powerful prayers and counsel of Sister Wilma, Elder Shirley, Lady Pat, Sister Connie, and our beloved Spiritual Mother Marietta.

I had to go to Fort Worth in July of 2018 for another claims certification. In all the drama and confusion, I met two ladies who worked with Delta and American Airlines. Stacey, a flight attendant for Delta, encouraged me to pursue a career as a flight attendant. She specifically directed me to Spirit Airlines. I was now 55 years old and had to seek God regarding this new direction for my life because I had been an Insurance Agent for over 28 years. It was my dream as a five-year-old to become a Flight Attendant, but I allowed that dream to die because I was only 5.2 feet tall. God resurrected that dream 50 years later. I felt a peace that surpassed any understanding to pursue a Flight Attendant career when I prayed about it. I again spoke to my WUTP leaders and asked for prayers. I applied to five different airlines, and would you believe Spirit Airlines wanted me to come out for an interview. I was not able to go because I had a claim in Alabama at the same time.

In December of 2018, I moved out of the friend's home and moved to Galveston, TX., not knowing where I will stay. I trusted God to take care of me and get me to "His Perfect Will" for my life. Sister Wilma, Elder Shirley, and Lady Pat would call me for updates about where I was living. I kept standing in faith until March 7, 2019, where I finally was led to the place I am staying now. It is the perfect place for me because it is affordable, five minutes from the beach, and I have a great neighbor named Kevin. He is a single black father with two adorable little girls named Kalani (4) and Leah (3). They always make me feel so loved and welcomed whenever they see me. God not only found me the perfect place to live but, He also blessed me with a brand new vehicle, and it was all done in one week after standing, waiting, praying, and declaring God's promises for 72 days. God was and still is so faithful to me. I realized that it all started after Hurricane Harvey, but I went into my 55 years of living and experienced double blessings for the entire year. WOW! ....God had turned my mourning into dancing, my weeping into joy, covered me with His Amazing Grace and His wonderful Favor. So I have to say that 2019 was my year of miracles!!!"

The beach is one of my favorite places, and I received a brand new 2019 Nissan Sentra. My family finally settled my late mother's sale of her condo after five years. I was able to visit my birthplace of Tobago and Trinidad after 46 years of being away, and I became a Flight Attendant for Spirit Airlines at the age of 56 on December 21, 2019. I accepted Spirits' second interview, and the whole interview process took approximately ten days. I now have a place in Galveston and Dallas, where Spirit Airlines has me based. Double Blessings!!! I love working for Spirit Airlines and the Holy Spirit. I partially love Spirit's uniform colors. They are black and yellow, just like the sun and bumblebee that is not supposed to fly. Sunny, bright, and cheerful for this new season of my life. I am so excited to have excellent health, 401K, and travel benefits. Most importantly, I get a chance to be a servant of the Most High God way up in the skies. It is the perfect second career for me if you know my personality.

It is 2020 now, and I am so excited to see what God has in store for my life. I genuinely believe all the twists and turns in the last three years led me to "God's Perfect Will" for my life because my heart is full of peace and joy in the Lord. If I had to go through all the drama I went through to get where I am today; I would do it all over again because it was worth it all!!! "God did exceedingly and abundantly more than I can ever ask, think, or imagine." Ephesians 3:20

In conclusion, I would not have made it through if it was not for my beautiful and anointed Prayer Angels at WUTP. I love and appreciate all your love, support, and, most importantly, your prayer covering. WUTP has meant the world to me for all seasons of my life. God Bless you!!!!! 😉

Sister Patricia "PattyCake" Pittman

Houston, Texas

I want to take this opportunity to thank Wake Up To Praise, especially Ms. Wilma Lofton, the person who was obedient to the voice of the Lord. He prompted her to bring her ministry to us who are part of WUTP and those who will be part of WUTP. This story is a condensed testament to my relationship with my Lord and Savior, Jesus Christ. I pray that you are enlightened! To all those whose eyes may glance across these pages, greeting, and salutations!!! My name is Sister Patricia "Pattycake" Pittman, and I am a new member of the Wake Up To Praise (WUTP) family. It has been a blessing to me, a lifeline.

I am 61 years young and married to my husband, Bernard. We have been married for 12 years, and God has truly blessed our marriage. I am a Private Duty Nurse who primarily does Home Health Care. I am also a Veteran of the United States Army. I guess if I have any gifts, that would be the gift of faith. I believe in God and the Bible, and I believe every word in it is TRUE. Also, I love to give. Giving makes my heart sing and smile. If I had a hobby, it would be servicing those in need, even to the point of sacrifice. I say this because I have learned that it's not about me during this journey, but it is all about God!! So now the journey. Where do I start? How about a little girl about five years old whose father had just left her. Just walked off, or I should say he ran off. My aunt had clunked him on the head with a large steel pipe and told him don't come back. He was abusive to my mom. Now it was just me, my brother, and my mama. I was glad he was gone, so he would not hit my mama, but I missed him too. I did not have big strong arms to run into to keep me safe or throw me up in the air. No lap to sit on or neck to hug. Yes, I did miss him, and mama had to work so hard. Then the unthinkable happened when I was 11 years old, my mother died. I was devastated and all alone. That is how I felt anyway.

We used to go to the country every summer when school was out to visit my grandparents. Me, my brothers and my cousins, we were all there. I loved it for the summer, but I did not want to live there now that my mom was gone. It was a safe place, but there was no indoor plumbing or running water. I could not take it, so I talked my grandparents into letting me stay in the city during my last year of grade school. It did not take long because I came running back to the country by the end of the year. I thought living in the city would be great. Boy, was I wrong!!! My relatives made me feel like a thrown away stepchild. Like Cinderella, so to speak, before she married the prince. It was awful, awful, awful.

I always felt so all alone. Everyone teased and ridiculed me. When I was home, my family would say, "You're so ugly. Look at your frog eyes and your big nose, just like your daddy. You ain't gonna be nothing, you gonna have a baby before you get out of high school." When I was at school, the kids would say, look at her. She wears the same old shoes every day or got on the same old clothes she had on the other day. I only had three changes of clothing, but they were always washed and ironed. I only had two pairs of shoes, one for school and one for church. "Look at her. I bet she stinks. She's so dumb. She's stupid." They laughed at me all the time.

No one wanted to be my friend or talk to me. I stood by the wall all alone. I had no one! My grandparents were religious people, and they made sure we went to church every Sunday. During Revival at church, all the kids had to sit and kneel on the mourner's bench. You kneel on that bench until you got saved. They told us that we had to pray to God and ask Him to save us so we wouldn't go to hell. For an entire week, we couldn't play, watch TV or listen to the radio. I did not understand the whole thing. I used to go out into the pasture behind our house, sit under the big tree near the pond, cry, and pour my heart out to God. A heart that was so hurt, broken, and unhappy. Though I did not know God, I would sit and talk to God all the time. He was the only one I could talk to. One day, I slept under the tree and had a dream that God saved me. When I went to church and told the Pastor and everyone what had happened, they all rejoiced that I was saved. There was no more mourner's bench for me. I could watch TV again, not that it mattered. I never got a choice of channels anyway.

Oh! By the way, we eventually got indoor plumbing and a bathroom with running water. That was great!!! Well, I graduated from High School with honors, obtained a scholarship, and went off to college that same summer. I did not want to wait. I was still looking for love in all the wrong places. I have done it all. I have lied, cheated, stolen, used to drink, and tried drugs of all kinds but never used the needle or shot up. I left college and went into the military and joined the US Army. After four years, I was discharged, went back home, stayed in the city, and worked to get established, but my heart was still so hurt and broken. I was so tired and unfulfilled.

I decided to try Jesus. At the age of 36, I gave my life to Christ. Here is where it all begins. I asked only one thing of Jesus. To show me that He is real, and boy, did He!!! He came in and fixed that old hurt and broken heart and gave me a new one. It feels brand new anyway. He gave me joy and peace, something I had been looking for all my life. More than that, He gave me love. He gave me love not just for me, but He made me understand that it's for everyone. My life is completely changed and different. Now my spiritual eyes have been opened, I can see!!! Jesus has given me everything. He has given me knowledge, wisdom, and understanding of His word. He has given me the Fruit of the Spirit, love, joy, peace, faith, goodness, kindness, gentleness, patience, and self-control.

My goodness, everything I have asked Him for, He has given it to me, and that's the truth. Even if some of those things were not good for me, He still gave them to me and helped me learn and grow from the consequences of those things that were not good for me. He is soooo good to me!!! He has given me much grace and favor, abundant and endless blessings! He is astounding, and if you let Him, He will blow your mind. He blessed me with the best job ever, working for a Jewish family. They were billionaires. God gave me such favor with the family. I worked with them and took care of their son for 11 years until we suddenly lost Lenny Dee, their son. I called him, "Dee." I loved him, so he was my heart. I took care of him just like he was my son. I did it with the love and high standards God admonishes us to do. Now I am 60 years old and have been working here for 11 years. What do I do? Where do I start? It was all so overwhelming. I did not think about it, but I thought I would retire in the back of my mind. After all, the other three nurses for twenty years retired. I had no idea that I would go back into the workforce at my age.

Resumes and filling out applications it was too much. I could not think clearly, and I was still grieving for "Dee" as well. Thank God for my Wake Up To Praise family. They saved me through it all. I asked Elder Shirley and the group to stand with me in prayer for a new job, one where I wouldn't have to walk on eggshells. A job where the family would be loving and kind. I still wanted to do home care but did not want to work in healthcare facilities. God did just that and then some!!! Again God has given me a great family to work with, and I love my little man Michael. He gave me another awesome family, which was more than I asked. It was beyond my expectations!

I declare with God All Things Are Possible! In The Name Of Jesus. Wake Up To Praise (WUTP) is a gift to me from God. I treasure my new family. It is a group of people from different states who get together by phone every Monday at 8:00 a.m. CST. They lift God and give Him praise and thanks for all that He has and is doing for them in their lives. They encourage me, they inspire me, and they provide me with strength! My spiritual eyes are now open, and I can see. I no longer walk around in the darkness. I give and will always give God All the Glory!!! AMEN.

Sister Sharon Haymon

Merrillville, Indiana

Mondays were my least favorite day of the week, mostly when I was in school. It continued to be my least favorite day of the week, and I used to have the Monday morning blues. That is until my dear sweet sister Wilma Brumfield-Lofton got the inspiration from the Holy Spirit to have a prayer group on Monday mornings, and my dear sweet Sister in Christ, Elder Shirley Rice, came up with the name, Wake Up To Praise. I thought that was the perfect name because it reminded me of my daddy, Mr. Samuel Peavy, who has gone home to be with the LORD.

When I was dragging in the mornings, he would always say, "Rise and shine and give GOD the glory," which is similar to Wake Up To Praise. Sometimes when I am discouraged, and things are not going right, and when I feel like not even getting out of the bed in the mornings, I remember what my daddy use to say, "Rise and shine and give GOD the glory... Rise and Shine!" Then I wake up praising the LORD for blessing my family, me, and another day to Praise HIM!!! My spirit is lifted to new heights, and then I know it will be a great day! Now I rise and shine every Monday morning to Wake Up To Praise. You, too, can experience the Wake Up To Praise phenomenon just by calling: 351-999-4991 at 8:00 CST.

You will be welcomed and greeted by a beautiful voice. Sometimes it is my beautiful sister Wilma Brumfield-Lofton, better known as "Lady Sparkle," my lovely sister in Christ, Avis Price, better known as "Bubbly," or my darling sister in Christ, Cleopatra Boone, better known as "Lady Pat." They always make you feel welcome and essential.

I also love and enjoy hearing our Spiritual Mother, Marietta Jordan, speak each Monday morning. She is so wise and inspirational and always seems to know just what to say. The Holy Spirit leads her. We then have scripture reading by our sister in Christ, the beautiful singing butterfly, Connie Smith, better known as "Queen Sparkle." She uplifts everyone each Monday morning with a scripture reading and a beautiful song, which is always refreshing and entertaining.

Then there is a segment called Praise Reports brought to you by our very own brother in Christ, Deacon Bobbie Stubblefield, who always says, "When prayers go up, blessings come down." This statement is so true! People call in to ask for prayer for whatever and whoever needs prayer.

The next segment is called Prayer Request, bought to you by my beautiful sister Wilma, better known as "Lady Sparkle." People get to share their testimonies of how GOD blessed and healed them after, sometimes during, the prayer segment. Like in my case a few years ago, I remember feeling very, very sick. I almost did not get on The Wake Up To Praise call because I was getting ready to go to the hospital. I was feeling weak and could hardly breathe. I had my three children at home, and I was babysitting three of my grandchildren, but I did not want to miss the Wake Up To Praise call. The children were very concerned, and I told them I was going upstairs to get ready to go to the hospital. I walked very slowly and carefully up the stairs. When I got upstairs, something told me to call the

Wake Up To Praise line. During the prayer request segment, having difficulty breathing, I asked for prayer. And amid Elder Shirley praying for me, I began to breathe easier and started to feel much, much better. GOD healed me that morning!!! When I got off the phone, I started singing and dancing around the house and praising HIS name! "Thank You, JESUS!!!" The children could not believe it, and they smiled to know that I was feeling better.

I know that there is so much power in prayer!!! Elder Shirley Rice is very anointed. She delivers such a powerful, soulful, heartfelt prayer until you can feel that power coming straight through the phone lines. She is an anointed vessel in which GOD reach and teach others through her. She prays for every caller, their prayer requests, and the problems in our country and worldwide. If you are still wondering if prayer works, I am a witness that prayer changes things, and if you do not believe me, I dare you to call Wake Up To Praise on Monday morning at 8:00 (CST); the number is 351-999-4991. Try it for yourself!!!

Recently we have incorporated a new segment where we learn about stories in the Bible. Someone chooses a topic, research it, and talks about it. It is very enlightening. Some topics so far included: "Fruit Of The Spirit," "Famous Men In The Bible," "Famous Women In The Bible," and so on. We have learned a lot from this segment, and sometimes we just let the Holy Spirit move and let GOD take the wheel. At those times, the spirit gets to moving!!! And one by one, callers speak from their hearts and souls.

It is very spiritual, very emotional, mighty, genuine, and very cleansing. GOD always knows just what we need!!! We end the call with a powerful anointed prayer by our very own sister in Christ, Elder Shirley Rice, better known as Our "Shero." Then we say our farewells until next Monday morning. The Wake Up To Praise experience leaves you feeling ready to face the week. But if you feel like you want a little bit more, please join us every Thursday evening at 7:00 (CST) for Bible study with our very anointed Pastor Morris Patterson and Elder Shirley Rice. The number is the same as the Wake Up To Praise number. Let us start the week off with Wake Up To Praise every Monday morning (8:00 CST). Wake Up To Praise is a sure cure for the Monday morning blues!!!

Praise GOD!!! Hallelujah and Amen!!! Be Blessed, Everyone!

Sister Avis "Bubbly" Price

Gary, Indiana

Growing up in Gary, IN, brings pleasant memories to my mind. Going to the movies at The Palace Theater, basketball games at Memorial Auditorium and football games at Gilroy Stadium were fun memories. These are hometown places that are no longer standing but are forever in my heart. I graduated from West Side High School in 1971. A true Cougar to heart! I attended Indiana State University in Terre Haute, IN, for a year after that. Shortly after that year, at the age of 19, I suffered a devastating spinal cord injury. My doctors told me that I would be paralyzed and confined to a wheelchair for life.

With physical therapy and the help and support from my family, I accepted my diagnosis and became independent. I became active in my community, working with The Council For Disability Rights by going to meetings to ensure that legislation passed and was up to date on transportation. It keeps me active and involved.

I am a stay at home mother and grand-mother. I have two beautiful adult daughters Tonya and Ashley. Tonya lives in Orlando, Florida, and Ashley resides here with me. I have three grand-daughters. Tia, Tamara, and Ayla. Tamara is a member of The U.S Army Stationed in Fort Bragg in North Carolina. Tia just graduated from high school in Orlando, Florida (virtually) because of the pandemic of 2020! My youngest, Ayla, is two and one half years old, living with me, and keeping me busy every day. 😄 They are my pride and joy.

I grew up in a church here in Gary with sisters Wilma Lofton and Juanita Green from a young age. Sister Lofton invited me to join Wake Up To Praise several years ago. I am ever grateful to her for that remarkable invite! I was affectionately given the nickname "Bubbly" by my dear friend Lady Pat. I take pride in being able to join my sisters and brothers in Christ. Monday mornings for the Wake Up To Praise call with Sister Wilma Lofton, Thursday evening Bible study with Pastor Morris Patterson and Elder Shirley Rice, and now on Sunday mornings as a new member of Belmount Missionary Baptist Church under the Leadership of the Honorable Pastor Morris Patterson and Lady Pamela Patterson of Memphis, TN. My cup is now filled. Each day I wake up to see another day is all praises to God our Father. I am blessed to have a family that loves me and friends from Wake Up To Praise who I love like family! May everyone's day be filled with peace, love, favor, and blessings!!

I Love You All!!! Bubbly 🖤 💕🙏

Praise Report..

I'm excited to share my praise report! As the weekend of the first Wake Up To Praise Retreat approached, my home health nurse gave me my recent health test results. She said I would have to be hospitalized that week and may need surgery. I thought about how much I planned and wanted to attend the Retreat. I was given the OK to attend but assured I had to be at the hospital on Monday for admission. The Retreat was wonderful! During the evening, my friend Sister Wilma Lofton asked our dear Elder Shirley Rice to Pray for me before I go to the hospital on that Monday. I can't explain the feeling that I felt as Elder Shirley prayed for me that evening. It was comfort and joy, as if I had no more worries. I felt the presence of God from her comforting words that day. Upon returning home, I had my bag ready and packed for the hospital stay. I called to see what time did they want me there. The nurse told me that I did not need to come because my test results showed no infection, and I was fine. I said, "What?" Nothing but God, I thought. I was covered by His blood. Thank you, God, for your blessings. Thank you, Elder Shirley, and the Wake Up To Praise family, for your prayers. Continue to keep me lifted in your prayers. There Is Power In Prayer! May God holds each and everyone in his protective arms.

I Love You All! Sister Avis (Bubbly) 🖤 🖤

Sister Joycelyn Tucker

Gary, Indiana

I knew of God when I was a little girl being raised in a devout Christian family. My maternal grandfather was a minister in the Church of God in Christ. My relationship went from just knowing God to knowing who and what He is in my life. This revelation happened when my husband Percy and I united with the Liberty Baptist Church in Gary, IN, under the leadership of the late Rev. Dr. Donald J. Starks Sr. It was at Liberty that we both matured in our relationship with Christ.

After joining Liberty, we became very close to and learned a great deal from Evangelist Shirley Rice. Through our conversations and fellowship, her Sunday School teaching and our working together in multiple ministries of the church gave us both a better understanding of God's Word, and I also gained a "sister!!"

One day my "sister" invited me to call into the Wake Up To Praise prayer line. This ministry was established by Sister Wilma Lofton and named by Minister Rice, my dear friend. I believe that when you take the time to look back over your life, you can see how God places people in your path. You do not know who, why, and for what purpose. But God knows!

Before and during this time, my husband's health began to fail him. He eventually had to retire from his job and go on disability. The illness was a difficult transition for him, not only because of his health issues but because he had been a hard working person from the time he was 15 years old. There were so many doctors and appointments. So many medications and hospital stays. There were even some surgeries. Of course, there were sleepless nights as we weathered this storm in our lives. As I stood by Percy's side, God sustained me. Now I know it was nobody but God and His keeping power. He had also placed these "Angels" in my life. Wake Up To Praise had not only grown in numbers but had also become a viable instrument of God's Love. I had established a bond with some incredible, strong, praying women of God!

Then one of the most significant tests of my faith occurred. My husband suffered a stroke, which left him unable to walk or talk. After a lengthy hospital stay, Percy was transferred to a long term nursing facility. He remained there for about 15 months before I was able to bring him home and care for him. Percy was at home for six months before his health began to decline again. Now there were more hospital stays, then a return to nursing home care. On May 1, 2019, my husband of 44 years, the first and only love of my life, made his transition. I held his hand as he took his last breath and joined his hand with God.

I know for a certainty that God kept me during this storm in my life, just as He continues to keep me each day. I also realized that He had already placed the beautiful people from Wake Up To Praise in my life. And they were always there for me day and night, praying with me and for me. They called and sent food, flower, cards, and letters of encouragement. These "Angels," most of whom I only knew by their voices, surrounded me with love and prayers. There are not enough words in the English language to express how much being a part of this ministry has meant in my life thus far. All I can do is thank God for His infinite wisdom, grace, and mercy. He knows that many of the women close to me have gone on to Glory. So God sent Wake Up To Praise to fill the void in my life.

According to His Purpose, may God always bless Minister Shirley Rice, Sister Wilma Lofton, and all the members of Wake Up To Praise in everything that they do or say for the Glory of God. AMEN!

Sis. Joycelyn Tucker

Memphis, Tennessee

Sister Julia Peavy

The Monday Wake Up To Praise call is a great way to start the week. Filled with inspiration, rejuvenation, and prayer. There is POWER IN PRAYER!!! I had been experiencing shoulder pain for quite some time. One Monday morning, as Elder Shirley was praying, I placed my hand on my shoulder. When I got off the prayer call, the pain was gone entirely. To God Be The Glory!!! Elder Shirley puts her heart, mind, and soul into her prayers of healing, intercession, petition, and supplication. During the Praise Report time on Monday morning, it is a joy to hear all the different praise reports of healing, prosperity, and sometimes miracle blessings! Every Thursday evening, we are empowered with "God's Good News" by Pastor Morris Patterson and Elder Shirley on our Bible study call. We gain knowledge, spiritual growth, and understanding collectively through their outstanding teaching. We have a segment where we can ask questions, which allows us to get more in-depth knowledge from our text. I am so proud to be a part of the Wake Up To Praise family. They are a loving, caring, giving group always sending cards, gifts, love tokens, etc. Every member's birthday or anniversary is acknowledged! The Wake Up To Praise Retreat was phenomenal!!! It started with The Circle Of Prayers and a powerful message by Pastor Antwon Brown and prayer by Minister Adrienne Watson. There was a trip to St. John, Indiana, and The Shrine Of Christ's Passion, where the group took the journey experiencing the story of the crucifixion and resurrection of Christ. Saturday evening was the awards dinner and Candle Lighting Ceremony. It was excellent!!! Many awards were given away, the entertainment and food were fabulous! Pastor Artrice Kennedy delivered a strong message, and Minister Leo Lavender ended the evening with an anointed prayer. We had a glorious time! I thank God that my daughter Wilma listened to the Holy Spirit and start this anointed group in January 2016. I pray that God will continue to bless and empower our wonderful Wake Up To Praise family.

Sister Denise Bowlin-Shaffer

Houston, Texas

My prayer is that my testimony touches someone's heart and mind and help them overcome any obstacle or challenge they might have. Because of fears about life's uncertainties, I have been a part of Wake Up To Praise since 2016. I am so fortunate. Every Monday morning, I wake up and give honor and praise to God together with all the blessed saints in our family. There is peace in their presence that surpasses all understanding. I have the confidence to say my Wake Up to Praise family will walk with me and be there whenever I fall to lift me. What a comfort knowing they are there in these trying times, with such darkness in this world.

My Wake Up To Praise family helped me overcome my challenges, fears, shame, guilt, and self-condemnation. They helped me see that God grants me my peace and my serenity to accept the things I cannot change, the courage to change the things I can, and the wisdom to know the difference. With constant prayers and support of my Wake Up To Praise warriors, I feel I can do all things with God. I have matured and blossomed into a new creature in Christ. A reborn, delivered, and refreshed woman of God, transformed with the renewing of my mind. I received so much of the love and support I never had before. This family walked with me, supported me, spoke life into my very being, and held me up until I could walk alone. I am every so grateful!!! The Wake Up To Praise family provides a constant prayer for the sick and shut-in and rest for the weary. They can come into our group and rest. WUTP helps you recharge your spirit to build you back up. A refreshing is needed to replenish your soul and spirit. They are the treasures of the heart and God's gifts to us for seeking his face daily. God has truly blessed me to be in such a loving environment in such a time like this. Our Wake Up to Praise family truly brings heaven to earth every day.

I have many experiences of overcoming health challenges, but the most recent one I want to share with you right now is my triumphant overcoming diabetes. One doctor told me I would have diabetes for life. I did not accept her diagnosis. I have had this diagnosis for over ten years and had many challenges trying to overcome this disease. I prayed to God for wisdom and revelation on how to overcome this challenge. Finally, I began to recognize the foods I was eating that raised my blood sugar. My sugar reading would be in the two hundred's every day. I completely changed my eating habits with God's power, not in my strength, because my obstacles were too overwhelming at that time. The doctor took me off the Metformin medication (500mg twice daily) that I had been taking for over ten years. My blood sugar reading is in the normal range now eighty or ninety, never over one hundred and forty. I feel good to have this freedom in truly knowing my body and what to eat in the right combinations. I can only say, "But God!!!" I Bless His Holy name, Jehovah-Rapha, my Healer and the One who makes bitter experiences sweet. You sent Your Word and healed me. You forgave all my iniquities, and You healed all my diseases. Hallowed Be Thy Name.

This is what the "Wake Up to Praise" family means to me:

W - We worship God together.

U - We have unity in faith together.

T - We have treasures of the heart that only God can give.

P - Our group provides peace of mind, prosperity to prosper as our soul prospers.

F - Faith to know God's presence to refresh you, His healing to restore you, God's strength to renew you.

Aberdeen, Mississippi

Sister Jacqueline Gunn

I was truly blessed when Mother Louise Jones invited me to join the Monday morning Wake Up To Praise call for prayer. Mother Jones's former Pastor, who was my husband, had brain surgery. Three days later, the doctors informed me he only had a two percent chance to live. I did not hesitate to tell him I hear you, "BUT GOD!" I am going to do what mother Jones says, "Trust in God." He said, "Lady, I admire your faith." When the Doctors say no, but God says, Yes! In my heart, mind, soul, and spirit, I kept telling myself this is a sabbatical moment and God will raise him off this death bed for the benefit of those watching and not believing there is a God and He is still in the miracle blessing business. Being connected with my Wake Up To Praise family strengthened me beyond measure. I walked that walk, knowing, trusting, and believing that My God was and still is faithful. I felt it was a test of my faith and belief because I was raised by parents who were preachers. Through it all, I found consolation in knowing that Jesus will never leave me alone. God may not show up on your time, but God is always on time. I am a witness. God will do what no other power can do. The Bible tells us how Jesus raised the dead, made the lame walk, and the blind to see. If He did all that, then I am a firm believer He can do that and more.

It was on my birthday, May 4, 2018, that I was determined to get this walking miracle to the Retreat in Indiana to meet my Wake Up To Praise family. On May 5, we walked into the formal setting, and when they realized we were the Gunn's, the whole atmosphere changed. They had finally put a face to the voices, and here comes the miracle!!! My two words going through this trial and test was "But God!!" There was an author there at the reunion by the name of Pastor Artrice Kennedy doing a book singing titled "But God!!" What a miracle!!!

When you need someone to pray for you and with you, call Wake Up To Praise!

"J E S U S is the Best 2020 Vision Just Trust Him and Wake Up To Praise God Daily"

Sister Connie "Queen Sparkle" Smith

Houston, Texas

Being a part of the Wake Up to Praise family has been one of the most life-changing experiences on my faith journey. I have grown by leaps and bounds in understanding what God has for me. I have learned to listen to the Holy Spirit at work in my life. God does speak, and I am blessed knowing this. I have heard on the WUTP call lives changed and how the favor of God truly works. People have been healed as we come together and pray because prayer is power. The enlightenment of God's love for us shines brightly daily. Knowing this fact causes such joy to be in His service for me, my family, friends, and anyone in my daily walk. Touching lives through Jesus, I can not go wrong.

There are so many life lessons, gifts from God, to share for the lightening of someone's life (day). I am so grateful for the privilege of being a core group member of Wake Up to Praise. This family, called Wake Up to Praise, never stops sharing, caring, praying, and lifting others in prayer. I pray that whoever is reading this message now will be inspired to be all you can be in Jesus' service. I am to be a fruit inspector. God has given us good fresh, delicious fruit to share. Through our sharing of our fruit, God's love shines, and blessings flow. As we continue humbly in our faith journey, there will be times when we may feel weak. The Holy Spirit directs me, lifts me to realize our Lord and Savior died for "even me." Then joy comes; I feel strong in Him. He is my strength. Anything good in me is the Jesus that lives in my heart. He is my constant companion who only wants the best for me. I know I can not "just do it" without Him.

On this Jesus journey, I have found that showing gratitude and being grateful for all things big and small, and remembering everything in my day/life begins and ends with God. Blessings we can not see, and the ones that are happening right now for the future is all good in Jesus. Be happy with what we have. When we wake up each day, it is another day to praise Him. If we do not wake up, praise Him as we return to the presence of God, WE WIN!! WE WIN!! WE WIN!!! Having faith in good times and bad is a powerful life lesson and a real blessing. Being filled with prayer and passion causes joyful, loving, gracious gifts when we continue every day following in Jesus' footsteps. "When we do, we share, we care and we live as brothers and sisters of faith… in Jesus." All, Glory and Honor to God Almighty.

Sister Connie Queen Sparkle Smith

Sister Virginia Campbell Maddox

Orlando, Florida

Wake Up To Praise is a top priority in my life. No matter what I have experienced on the weekend, I dial 351-999-4991 at 8:00 A.M. Central Standard Time or 9:00 A.M. Eastern Standard Time to communicate with my sisters and brothers in Christ. During the call, we share our testimonies from the answered prayer requests petitioned to our Father. "And this is the confidence that we have in him, that, if we ask any thing according to his will, he heareth us; and if we know that he hear us, whatsoever we ask, we know that we have the petitions that we desired of him." 1 John 5:14-15. We pray with our confidence in God, believing that He will hear and answer our prayers. According to His divine plan, do not demand that He give us what we want but to perform His perfect will in our lives. We are blessed with the founder and host of Wake Up To Praise, Wilma "Lady Sparkle" Lofton. God has anointed her with a cheerful heart and an encouraging eloquent voice that will lift your spirit as she welcomes you to Wake Up To Praise. Our Spiritual Mother, Marietta Jordan, gives us a word of wisdom and encouragement. Elder Shirley Rice, our "She-Ro," our "Prayer Warrior," prays for us. Remember that Matthew 18:18 & 19 tells us that, "Verily I say unto you, Whatsoever ye shall bind on earth shall be bound in heaven: and whatsoever ye shall loose on earth shall be loosed in heaven. Again I say to you, That if two of you shall agree on earth, as touching any thing that shall ask, it shall be done for them of my Father which is in heaven." If you need love, support, and want to grow stronger in God, come and join us. You will be glad you did!

Your Sister In Christ,

Virginia Campbell Maddox

Canton, Ohio

Sister Teesa M. Smith-Stewart

My name is Teesa M. Smith-Stewart, and my mother, Connie Smith, introduced me to Wake Up To Praise in the summer of 2019.

She may not know this, but she introduced me to a real awakening in my life. Being a part of WAKE UP TO PRAISE has TRULY been a blessing in my life. I thought I knew joy............ But, I must say there is no joy like the joy I found in all my new sisters and brothers in Christ I found on this prayer line.

It was as if the flood gates were opened in my life. I have received blessings upon blessings since I have become a part of souls like mine. This group has taught me how to live by the scripture Ephesians 6:11. "Put on the whole amour of God, that ye may be able to stand against the wiles of the devil." I have found nothing more than peace and happiness since joining the group. I thank God for my mother because she cared enough to share you all with me.

THANK GOD FOR YOU ALL AND PRAISE THE LORD FOR HIS BLESSINGS .....AMEN.

Missouri City, Texas

Sister Helen Brown

One day, I was given a Wake Up To Praise flyer by Wilma Lofton. I placed it on the dining room table, and several weeks later, I decided to call the number. The discussion was very insightful, and I truly enjoyed it. I also loved the Bible study on Thursday night. My niece developed a severe diabetic foot infection, and the doctor told her she needed her foot amputated. She refused. I asked the Wake Up To Praise family to pray for her foot to heal. I made this request each week. The Wake Up To Praise family continued to pray to Jesus, our Lord, and Savior, to heal her foot. Several months later, my niece's foot healed. This healing was a miracle and a blessing from Jesus! One day, the person who usually conducts the Praise Report could not participate because of a doctor's appointment. Wilma asked me to fill in for him. I was honored to lead the Praise Reports. I truly felt I belonged to this Wake Up To Praise family! "To God Be The Glory"

The Wake Up To Praise Retreat

The WUTP Retreat was beaming with excitement from the beginning to the end! The registration packets were picked up that Friday. They contained a tote bag, polo shirt, cap, etc. Everyone got a chance to meet and greet, putting faces to the voices, finally meeting for the very first time in person! On Saturday morning, we held our Circle Of Prayers, where Pastor Antwon Brown delivered a powerful and inspiring message! Minister Adrienne Watson administered Communion and spoke an anointed prayer over all the prayer requests. After the Circle of Prayers, the bus took our group to St. John, Indiana, to the Shrine Of Christ's Passion. It was an exciting journey through the stunning shrine displaying the Passion Of Christ, which contained 40 life-size statues depicting the time from the Agony in the Garden to the Resurrection.

Saturday evening was our magnificent awards dinner, and the entertainment was Those Funny Little People. A one-of-a-kind entertainment company with life-sized puppets who sing, dance, and make people laugh. They were hilarious!!! The dinner was absolutely delicious! Pastor Artrice Kennedy shared an empowering message, and her husband, Pastor Richard Kennedy, also shared some empowering words. We had several miracle blessings to happen! A couple surprised us by showing up at the awards dinner. The husband had been in the hospital for several weeks and was very ill. We did not think they would attend the Retreat, so when we saw them walk through the door, we clapped and cheered with joy! There was another miracle blessing. One member was supposed to be admitted to the hospital the Monday after our Retreat for treatment and possible surgery. I asked Elder Shirley if she would pray for her and she spoke a powerful prayer of healing. That Monday, she was told by her doctor that she would not have to be admitted. TO GOD BE THE GLORY!

Minister Leo and his lovely wife Betty were celebrating his birthday that weekend! Those Funny Little People and our WUTP family sang the happy birthday song, we had cake and presented him with a gift. Awards were presented to WUTP members, and at the end of the program, we had our Candle Light Ceremony. It was very touching. We then closed out the evening with a prayer by Minister Leo. Sunday morning Pastor Richard & Artrice Kennedy, along with some other WUTP members, attended the Worship Service at Liberty Baptist Church. Elder Shirley Rice & her husband Larry, Deacon Stubblefield & his wife Nicole, and Sister Joycelyn Tucker are members under Pastor Antwon Brown & Lady Jennifer's leadership.

We're all are looking for our next WUTP Retreat!!!

Retreat

Retreat

Retreat

Gone But Not Forgotten

We will cherish your memories

Iceal Peavy

Mother Iceal Peavy was a faithful and God-fearing woman of God who truly loved the Lord and all God's children. She would weekly share with me during our daily, and weekly phone calls her experience and love for the Wake Up To Praise Bible study line/calls. She would always share how rich and good the Word of God was and how the "Dynamic Duo" Pastor Patterson and Elder Shirley would carefully and rightly dissect and break down the Word of God every Thursday evening that she was able to dial on the line. She always said the Word of God was so captivating, and "The reading of the scriptures that she had heard and read for so many years seems to shed new light and life to the Word of God as her eyes of understanding begin to see even clearer." She enjoyed the comfort of relaxing at home in her bedroom, not having to worry about finding someone to take her to church for Bible study, trying to find something to wear, or having to deal with a walker to get about from place to place.

All she had to do was locate her handy phone book with all of her important phone numbers, get her glasses, which were most of the time on her face or nearby, and her pad and paper to write down some key points or scriptures. Although her natural eyesight was not as sharp as it had been, her spiritual eyesight and her natural and spiritual ears remained open and attentive to the Word of God shared weekly by the "Dynamic Duo" and others who had powerful testimonies and remarks. We are so grateful for her lovely niece and our loving cousin Wilma. A woman of excellence, zeal, and so much love for the Lord who introduce Mother Peavy (affectionately known as Aunt Iceal) to the Wake Up To Praise family, not sure what year she started. After her first call to a Thursday Bible study, she was hooked for life until her failing health prevented her from making the weekly calls in 2019. She would always encourage me to dial in on the Bible study line weekly, but my church's Bible study was on the same night weekly, 6-8 pm in Virginia. Sometimes I would catch the end of the call. I would get a chance to connect with her on the line if Bible study was canceled.

Cousin Wilma and her siblings would weekly, on Sunday, call Auntie Iceal on the phone whether she was home, in the hospital, or rehab center to say hello, encourage her and tell her they loved and missed her. She would always tell me about her calls with them, and her children inspired her daily. She would be so refreshed and renewed after the weekly Bible study calls. She would be so excited to share what was discussed and shared on the call when she and I would talk. She loved receiving all the calls, cards, gifts, and unconditional love from the Wake Up To Praise family when she was sick and doing well. She was so excited to attend her only Wake Up To Praise Retreat in the Spring of 2017/18 in Indiana. She got a chance to attend with her loving and only daughter Jacinta and baby son Julian. They both enjoyed their mother's joy and happiness, finally uniting with the Wake Up To Praise family. She loved the fellowship, the real and unconditional love and concern they all showed. She was so excited to share her testimony with the WUTP family about how the Lord completely healed her from colon

44 | Wake Up To Praise: Gone But Not Forgotten

cancer as it was in complete remission. I am sure she shared her many testimonies of healing with the Wake Up To Praise family. She loved the opportunity to finally put a face with a name and voice at the WUTP Retreat that weekend. She was unable to make the trip to the Saturday tour to St John, Indiana, visiting the city of Jerusalem because of all the walking. She did not have a faithful wheelchair, so her loving niece Wilma stayed and kept her

company back at the hotel with her sis-in-law, Aunt Julia. I am sure they had a lovely time and fellowship together.

The Wake Up To Praise family has always embraced Aunt/Mother Iceal Peavy as one of their very own. I am sure she loved meeting Spiritual Mother, her covenant sister, and all the others as well. The Lord and His Word have always been the cornerstone and foundation of Mother Peavy's walk of faith here on earth. The Lord saw fit to graduate her to heavenly rest last year on August 2, 2019. She is resting in heavenly peace as we continue to carry on her legacy and love for the Lord and His Kingdom and all God's children. We eternally love and thank the Wake Up To Praise family for always being there for our loving Mother. May God continue to bless and keep you all in His perfect will and peace. We love you all to eternal and abundant life!!

Elder Marlon Peavy and Family

My mom looked forward to being on the WUTP Bible Studies call every Thursday evening. I listened to many of the Bible studies with her. I also attended the WUTP Retreat with mom. She enjoyed it, and so did I!

Jacinta Peavy

I had a great time attending the Wake Up To Praise Retreat with my wonderful Mother and two of my siblings. It was a joy and pleasure seeing my Mother enjoying her Wake Up To Praise family, finally meeting many of them in person for the first time. There was so much love, fun, and excitement during the entire Retreat! Mother Peavy received two trophies and spoke at the awards dinner. She shared her testimony of how she was diagnosed with cancer in 2012, and now she was cancer free. I am so glad I took time out of my schedule to be at the Wake Up To Praise Retreat with my mother, another memory that I will always cherish!

Julian Peavy

My wife Annette and I attended the Wake Up To Praise Retreat. We enjoyed the entire weekend! It was Awesome seeing my Mother have such a great time with her Wake Up To Praise sisters and brothers. My mother often talked about the Wake Up To Praise calls. I'm glad my cousin Wilma invited my Mother to be a member of this loving group of Christian believers.

Duaine Miller

Gone But Not Forgotten
We will cherish your memories

Pastor Artrice Kennedy

Pastor Artrice Kennedy was a blessing to our Wake Up To Praise family. She spoke on several of our Thursday evening Bible study calls, blessed and empowered us sharing God's Good News! Pastor Artrice & Pastor Richard Kennedy are the Authors of the book BUT GOD! We were able to purchase their book at our Retreat. Pastor Artrice delivered a powerful message at our Awards Night. Pastor Artrice & Pastor Richard celebrated their 54th Wedding Anniversary on April 29, 2020. May 8, 2020, was Pastor Artrice's birthday; she passed from this life six days later, on May 14, 2020. We cherish and thank God for the Legacy that she left with us! We will keep Pastor Richard Kennedy and family in our prayers! We love you! God Bless You All!

Gone But Not Forgotten
We will cherish your memories
Lady Frances Fulton-Hart

Lady Frances Fulton-Hart was a charter member in Wake Up To Praise until 2018. Lady Fran's schedule became busy, helping her husband, Pastor Hart, with programs and other church activities. Frances was a dedicated wife, mother, and grandmother.

We cherish the fond memories of the time that France spend as a member of Wake Up To Praise.

Our Prayers are with her loving husband and family.

Printed in the United States
By Bookmasters